D1177414

VIZ GRAPHIC NOVEL

CERES
Celestial Legend
Vol. 4: Chidori

Story and Art by
YUU WATASE

CERES™
Celestial Legend
Volume 4: Chidori
Shôjo Edition

This volume contains the CERES: CELESTIAL LEGEND installments
from Part 4, issue 1, through Part 4, issue 4, in their entirety.

STORY & ART BY YUU WATASE

English Adaptation/Gary Leach
Translation/Lillian Olsen
Touch-up Art & Lettering/Melanie Lewis
Cover Design & Layout/Hidemi Sahara
Editor — 1st Edition/Andy Nakatani
Shôjo Edition Editors/Elizabeth Kawasaki & Frances E. Wall

Editor in Chief, Books/Alvin Lu
Editor in Chief, Magazines/Marc Weidenbaum
VP of Publishing Licensing/Rika Inouye
VP of Sales/Gonzalo Ferreyra
Sr. VP of Marketing/Liza Coppola
Publisher/Hyoe Narita

Printed in Canada

Published by VIZ Media, LLC
P.O. Box 77010
San Francisco CA 94107

Shôjo Edition

10 9 8 7 6 5 4 3 2

First printing, July 2004
Second printing, July 2007
First English edition, May 2003

www.viz.com
store.viz.com

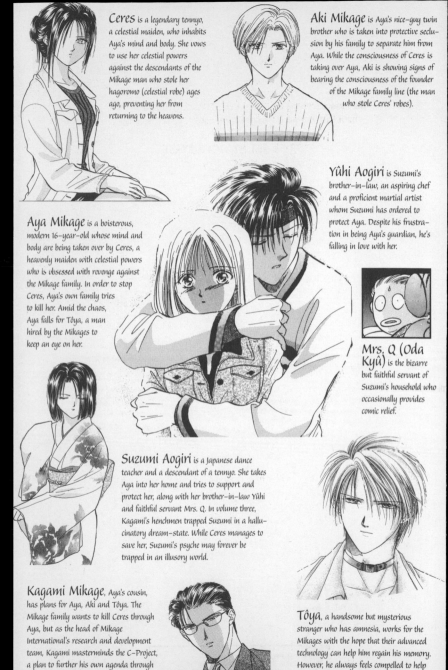

Ceres is a legendary tennyo, a celestial maiden, who inhabits Aya's mind and body. She vows to use her celestial powers against the descendants of the Mikage man who stole her hagoromo (celestial robe) ages ago, preventing her from returning to the heavens.

Aki Mikage is Aya's nice-guy twin brother who is taken into protective seclusion by his family to separate him from Aya. While the consciousness of Ceres is taking over Aya, Aki is showing signs of bearing the consciousness of the founder of the Mikage family line (the man who stole Ceres' robes).

Yûhi Aogiri is Suzumi's brother-in-law, an aspiring chef and a proficient martial artist whom Suzumi has ordered to protect Aya. Despite his frustration in being Aya's guardian, he's falling in love with her.

Aya Mikage is a boisterous, modern 16-year-old whose mind and body are being taken over by Ceres, a heavenly maiden with celestial powers who is obsessed with revenge against the Mikage family. In order to stop Ceres, Aya's own family tries to kill her. Amid the chaos, Aya falls for Tôya, a man hired by the Mikages to keep an eye on her.

Mrs. Q (Oda Kyû) is the bizarre but faithful servant of Suzumi's household who occasionally provides comic relief.

Suzumi Aogiri is a Japanese dance teacher and a descendant of a tennyo. She takes Aya into her home and tries to support and protect her, along with her brother-in-law Yûhi and faithful servant Mrs. Q. In volume three, Kagami's henchmen trapped Suzumi in a hallucinatory dream-state. While Ceres manages to save her, Suzumi's psyche may forever be trapped in an illusory world.

Kagami Mikage, Aya's cousin, has plans for Aya, Aki and Tôya. The Mikage family wants to kill Ceres through Aya, but as the head of Mikage International's research and development team, Kagami masterminds the C-Project, a plan to further his own agenda through the descendants of tennyo.

Tôya, a handsome but mysterious stranger who has amnesia, works for the Mikages with the hope that their advanced technology can help him regain his memory. However, he always feels compelled to help Aya escape dangerous situations.

CERES! CAN'T *YOU* DO SOMETHING?!

CAN'T *YOU* SNAP HER OUT OF THIS HYPNOSIS?!

I CANNOT.

...SUZUMI!!! C'MON, WAKE UP!!

...KAZUMA...

SHE CAN ONLY COME OUT OF IT BY HER OWN CHOICE.

SHE ENTERED THIS DREAM WILLINGLY...

UM...

YOU CAME HERE... TO THIS HOUSE BY *YOUR* OWN CHOICE, DIDN'T YOU?

YEAH, OKAY! JUST LET ME ATTEND TO YOUR WOUND...

IT'S NOTHING. SEE TO SUZUMI...

FATHER! YOU'RE *WOUNDED!* I'D BETTER CALL AN AMBULANCE...

DON'T YOU UNDERSTAND?

FATHER...

WHY... DID YOU PROTECT ME...?

IT'S A FATHER'S DUTY... TO PROTECT HIS CHILDREN.

DON'T YOU GET IT, YŪHI?

FATHER'S ALWAYS...

THOUGHT A LOT OF *YOU*...

BUT THAT CAN'T... I MEAN, HOW CAN *THAT* JUSTIFY *YOU* LIVING WITH SUZUMI UNDER THE *SAME ROOF*?!

?!

I KNOW IT'S PETTY, BUT YOU ALWAYS MADE ME FEEL JEALOUS... THAT BUSINESS OF THE POOR, ABANDONED URCHIN, TUGGING AT THE HEARTSTRINGS.

HMPH...

6

♦ Chidori ♦

UH... AND WHERE DID AYA *GO?*

...

DON'T BE RIDICULOUS!!

OOH!!

OH!!

THE *CRAZY, SALACIOUS THINGS* YOU MUST BE GETTING TO DO *EACH AND EVERY DAY!* "C'MON SUZUMI!" "OH YŪHI, WE MUSTN'T..."!!

AKK!!

OOH!!

AYA... YOU LET CERES EMERGE FOR *OUR* SAKE...

AND NOW, *AYA* IS THROWN INTO THE *BARGAIN!!*

Idiot...

...I WANT A *BOY...* JUST LIKE YOU, KAZUMA.

WHAT... DO *YOU* THINK ...?

IT WASN'T ME!!

YŪHI! I KNEW IT! I KNEW IT!

STOMP STOMP STOMP STOMP

SHE WAS... PREGNANT...

WHAT'S SHE TALKING ABOUT?

LIAR! KAZUMA'S BEEN *GONE* FOR OVER A *YEAR!* WHO ELSE *COULD* HAVE...?!

THE BABY... ISN'T THERE... ANYMORE.

HUH?

STOMP STOMP STOMP

SHE DOESN'T WANT TO COME BACK... TO REALITY. SHE WOULD RATHER STAY IN THAT BYGONE WORLD WITH HER HUSBAND...

WITH THEIR CHILD ON THE WAY...THE HAPPIEST TIME SHE'S EVER KNOWN.

A BOY *OR* A GIRL-- EITHER WOULD BE GREAT.

AS LONG AS HE OR SHE IS HEALTHY...

NOTHING HERE IN THIS REALITY COULD BE MORE IMPORTANT TO HER THAN HER HUSBAND AND CHILD... SHE WILL NOT RETURN.

I LOVE YOU.

WOW... THREE MONTHS PREGNANT... THAT'S WONDERFUL, SUZUMI!!

...I HAD NO IDEA!!

SO *THAT'S* WHY SHE COLLAPSED AT KAZUMA'S FUNERAL...AND WAS IN THE HOSPITAL FOR TWO WEEKS...

•••

GLARE!

9

12

I LOST MY BIG BROTHER...!

SUZUMI...

OUT OF RESPECT FOR MOTHER, FATHER CAN'T LET HIS REAL FEELINGS FOR YŪHI SHOW...

HE'S STILL SO YOUNG, YET SO QUIET AND SO ALONE...

I'M ALL YŪHI HAS, THE ONLY ONE HE CAN TURN TO. ...I HAVE TO PROTECT HIM.

YŪHI... I HAVE TO... WATCH OVER HIM.

KAZUMA... *YOUR* LITTLE BROTHER IS *MY* LITTLE BROTHER.

"I WANT TO WATCH OVER HIM.. UNTIL HE'S GROWN UP."

SUZUMI!

SUZUMI...

"WATCH OVER HIM... IN MY PLACE..."

WELCOME BACK.

...YŪHI...

...ALL RIGHT... I UNDERSTAND.

14

CERES: 4

THE OPERATION FAILED. FUMBLING CLODS... I *WARNED* THEM NOT TO CAUSE A DISTURBANCE.

THE AOGIRIS HAVE POLITICAL CLOUT, AND COULD BE A REAL NUISANCE IF THINGS GET TOO PUBLIC.

beep

CHIEF?

THEN WE'LL HOLD OFF ON APPREHENDING SUZUMI AOGIRI...?

And that reminds me. I wonder how that weird-looking Mrs. Q is doing?

THEY WON'T BE SO STUPID AS TO TAKE US ON DIRECTLY... BUT NOW THEY KNOW SOMETHING'S UP, AND WILL BE ON THEIR GUARD.

SOME SETBACKS ARE TO BE EXPECTED.

ping

WE'RE TRYING TO ARTIFICIALLY "MANUFACTURE" CELESTIAL MAIDENS, SOMETHING THAT'S NEVER BEEN DONE BEFORE.

HEY YOU GUYS! WHAT'RE YOU DOING LETTING AKI OUT OF HIS ROOM WITHOUT OUR *PERMISSION?*

Bad guards! Bad!

AKI...!

...I REALLY WANTED TO SEE TŌYA...

I INSISTED.

I NEEDED TO...

WEEOO WEEOO WEEOO WEEOO

WHAT?! BUT--

THE POLICE... YŪHI! YOU AND THAT GIRL GO HOME, *NOW!*

LEAVE THE GROWN-UPS TO DEAL WITH THE AUTHORITIES. JUST GO HOME.

WEEOO WEEOO

JUST MAKE SURE YOU BRING AYA OR SUZUMI WITH YOU... Y'HEAR?

YŪHI... COME BACK TO SHOW US MORE OF YOUR CULINARY SKILLS.

IT'S ALL RIGHT, I'M FINE NOW.

KINDA PATHETIC, THOUGH... YOU'VE SAVED *ME* TWICE NOW...

IT'S OKAY... NOBODY'S KEEPING SCORE!

WATCH THE ROAD!

IT'S SO GOOD TO SEE YOU'RE ALL SAFE!

I WAS REAL CLOSE TO CALLING IN THE SELF-DEFENSE FORCES! ♫

OH, POOH! LOOK, NO HANDS!

STOP IT!

I GUESS... IF YOU JUST GET A GRIP AND DO WHAT YOU HAVE TO DO, THINGS CAN WORK OUT. YOU *CAN* MAKE A DIFFERENCE.

THIS FEELS SO... ANTI-CLIMACTIC.

I WAS ALL WIRED AND ANXIOUS ON THE WAY THERE...

"THE PEOPLE HERE... *ARE* MY FAMILY."

IF AYA HADN'T SAID THAT... I WOULD'VE MISSED SOMETHING IMPORTANT.

DON'T FORGET...

...OUR PROMISE...

STARE

EYES ON THE *ROAD*, MRS. Q!

OKAY...

FWIP

WHAT HAPPENED TO SUZUMI... AND YOUR DAD?!

TH- THEY'RE FINE! THANKS TO YOU...

I WAS JUST CHANGING YOU BACK FROM CERES...!

JRK...

STOP! IT'S NOT WHAT YOU... OUCH! OW!

YOU SLIMY LECH!

WHACK

SMACKK

PUNCH

UM, WE'RE HOME. YOU MIGHT WANT TO WRAP UP YOUR DISCUSSION.

PHEW

I'VE DECIDED...

DON'T THANK *ME*, THOUGH... THANK *CERES*.

TŌYA...

HOW ABOUT IT, TŌYA?

HAVE YOU THOUGHT ABOUT WHAT YOU WANT... YOUR MEMORY, OR AYA?

KAGAMI...

ME...?

THOSE CUFFS ARE RIDICULOUS. I'M TAKING THEM OFF.

AKI...

beep

I HEARD... THAT YOU'RE IN *LOVE* WITH AYA.

AKI INSISTED ON SPEAKING WITH YOU...

...

I CHOOSE AYA--

TŌYA!

I KIND OF FIGURED... I THINK SHE FEELS THE SAME ABOUT YOU.

THEY TOLD ME LOTS OF THINGS, ABOUT HOW YOU'VE BEEN PROTECTING HER AND ALL.

...

30

AYA IS MINE, AND MINE *ALONE!*

I WON'T LET YOU GET IN THE WAY...

IT'S BEEN PRE-DETERMINED. IT IS OUR DESTINY!

AKI...!

✦ Chidori ✦

Oh, I'd been thinking about how I said in a previous sidebar that **Ceres** is rather dark, and then I realized – this is a contemporary drama. I guess this is what happens when I try to set the story in the present day. The present day as I see it is gloomy and gray (at least Japan is). People as a whole, even children, are depressed. They look tired. Even high school girls, those hordes of look-a-like clones, who are said to represent the present day, look like they lack spirit to me and my assistants. It's like they're living a lie, without realizing it, by acting so incredibly chipper. But I guess it's okay, as long as they're having fun. And if I focus on that, the series is probably going to be really dark, but there are still lots of things that show it's not all bad for mankind. Also, those girls labeled kogals might look flighty on the outside,

but they could be pretty serious inside. Really?
It's not good when people just go by outward appearances. The media is making too much of a big deal. And there are way too many stupid adults around! Still, I hope young boys and girls don't lose heart. You can change the future. Each of you has that power. Wait until you are older to start thinking about the futility of it all. And I'll have Aya keep doing her best, too. This is an age when parents and children kill each other, and people with money and power use underhanded methods to get what they want. The Mikage Family is representative of those things for me. And as you may have realized, the theme is the same as my previous series. My next series will also probably inherit the same theme too. Just like genes.

COULD BE A SIDE EFFECT OF THE "MEMORY PROBE" APPARATUS. SURE, I DEVELOPED IT, BUT I'VE FOUND ITS ACTUAL EFFECTS ON THE HUMAN PSYCHE RATHER DIFFICULT TO PIN DOWN.

BUT WHAT HE DID TO TŌYA... THAT WASN'T NORMAL.

PERHAPS. WE'LL KEEP CLOSE WATCH... FOR THE TIME BEING...

...I'M HOME.

NO, SHE'S DOING "MATSU NO HAGOROMO - THE HAGOROMO ON THE PINE." IT'S HER FINEST ROUTINE!

"NO MATTER HOW THE WORLD MAY CHANGE, MINE HEART IS CONSTANT IN DEVOTION - MY CLOAK IS BLUSH'D WITH LOVE. THE PINETREE WHERE LOVERS' VOWS..."

IS SUZUMI GIVING A LESSON AT THIS HOUR?

"...NO, NO, I, TOO, AM A HEAVENLY MAIDEN..."

"...HAGOROMO..."?

I had no idea there was a dance like that.

"...LOOK, FLOWERS OF MARVELOUS FRAGRANCE FALL, AND THE FEATHER'D CLOAK OF HEAVEN BILLOWS..."

STARE

AYA! PLEASE, COME IN!

HAKURYO, THE MAN IN THIS SONG, SEES THE TENNYO IN TEARS, AND GIVES BACK THE ROBES HE HAD STOLEN. THE MAIDEN DANCES FOR HIM IN RETURN, AND THEN GOES BACK TO HEAVEN.

ABOUT THE SAME, THANKS. UM... I DIDN'T MEAN TO DISTURB YOU...

HOW IS YOUR MOTHER?

YOU DIDN'T. THIS ISN'T A DANCE YOU DO BY YOURSELF, ANYWAY.

MY DANCING PARTNER IS NO LONGER HERE... I HADN'T DANCED IT SINCE HE... WELL, UNLIKE THE SONG, MY BELOVED HAS GONE TO HEAVEN AND I REMAIN HERE...

...MY HEART FOREVER YEARNING...

YOU'RE... SO STRONG, SUZUMI...

HM?

I WANT TO BE GROWN UP ABOUT IT, BUT IF I'M WAVERING LIKE THAT... MAYBE I JUST *THINK* I'M IN LOVE.

ME, I GET ANXIOUS RIGHT AWAY IF... IF *MY* BELOVED ISN'T ALWAYS BY MY SIDE.

TO FEEL ANXIETY AND UNCERTAINTY IN THE FACE OF IT IS ONLY NATURAL.

I THINK... LOVE IS MANY THINGS, NONE OF THEM EASY TO UNDERSTAND. FOR ALL ITS WONDER, LOVE CHALLENGES YOU TO YOUR UTMOST.

WHEN I LOST MY HUSBAND AND CHILD... I CRUMBLED. I GAVE UP, LOST HOPE...

BUT NOW... I KNOW I HAVE TO ACCEPT AND CONFRONT MY FATE... AND NOT COWER IN SORROW.

TIPPY-TAP TIPPY-TAP TIPPY-TAP TIPPY-TAP

梧
AOGIRI

tip
tup

THE PREFECTURAL PUBLIC HEALTH DEPARTMENT, IN AN UNPRECEDENTED MOVE, DISTRIBUTED A VACCINE...

TOCHIGI...

HUH?

...A MYSTERIOUS PATHOGEN WAS FOUND IN TOCHIGI PREFECTURE...

EX-

YOU THINK I...? *GEEZ, GUYS...!*

heh GETTING A LITTLE LOLITA ACTION?

YŪHI, WHAT... IS YOUR INVOLVEMENT WITH THIS... CHILD?

SQUEEZE

GURF!

WHAT *IS* THIS?!

THIS IS GREAT! OOH, YOU'RE EVEN *COOLER* IN PERSON! ♥

GLARE

UH...

...THE WOMAN I SAW *FLYING* WITH YŪHI?!

AYA! WAIT!

HEY, ARE *YOU*...

WHOA, *THAT'S...!*

YOU SAW...?

LEMME GET A GOOD LOOK AT YOUR FACE!

I DON'T KNOW HER, NEVER EVEN *MET* HER! RIGHT, EVERYONE?!

WELL, YOU'VE FIGURED *WRONG!*

...

HUH? YOU SAY THAT AFTER ALL THE TIMES YOU'VE *KISSED* HER--

I TOOK THIS PICTURE WHEN I WAS AT THE SHINJUKU HOSPITAL THREE MONTHS AGO!

THEN THERE WAS THAT SCHOOL FIRE, AND YŪHI WAS ON TV AND ALL...AND I FIGURED I'D FIND *HIM* AND BE ABLE TO MEET *HER!*

THE WOMAN IN MY PICTURE IS A *BEAUTIFUL, ELEGANT GROWN-UP* WITH *LUXURIANT, FLOWING BLACK HAIR.*

SO I FINALLY SEE HER... CERES...

WAIT A MINUTE, IT'S NOT YOU!

MY OTHER SELF...

WAA-HEY

AYA!

IT'S NOT LIKE I *ASKED* TO BE CERES, IT JUST SORT OF *HAPPENED,* AND NOW WE'RE *STUCK* WITH EACH O...

WELL, EXCUSE ME!

YOU'RE JUST A TEENAGER WITH A STUPID DYE JOB.

TOCHIGI!?!

MY LITTLE BROTHER NEEDS YOU!

Tochigi...

..SO YOUR BROTHER FELL ILL FROM THIS PATHOGEN THEY FOUND, THE ONE THEY WERE TALKING ABOUT ON THE NEWS...

YEAH! MOST PEOPLE, INCLUDING ME, DIDN'T GET SICK BECAUSE WE TOOK THE MEDICINE THEY WERE GIVING OUT, BUT A FEW GOT SICK ANYWAY.

MY BROTHER'S BEEN IN THE HOSPITAL FOR THREE DAYS!

UH, YEAH... HI!

UMM...

SHŌTA! SHŌTA! I BROUGHT THE GIRL IN THAT PICTURE! SEE?

OH, THAT'S MRS. Q... EASY MISTAKE.

DOESN'T LOOK MUCH LIKE HER.

WOW! SHE'S THE ONE WHO WAS *FLYING*...?

A WHEELCHAIR...

YOU REALLY *DID* BRING HER! NEAT! BUT CAN SHE REALLY FLY?

LIKE A BIRD! WHEN I SAW HER, SHE WAS SOARING OVER A HIGH-RISE!

EASY MISTAKE...?!

52

54

IF I FACE MY PROBLEMS INSTEAD OF AVOIDING THEM...THEN WILL I ONE DAY BE ABLE TO BELIEVE, LIKE SUZUMI, THAT EVEN THE SAD TIMES...

...PREPARED ME FOR THE HAPPIEST MOMENTS I'LL HAVE AS A WOMAN...?

CERES IS THE ONE WHO CAN DO WHAT SHE ASKS.

I DON'T MIND, REALLY. THOUGH SHE'S SORT OF ASKING THE WRONG PERSON.

...ALL RIGHT. *WE'LL* CHECK OUT THE OTHERS HERE WHO MIGHT BE C-GENOMES.

GASP!

SO DON'T GET TOO STRESSED OUT, OKAY?

WITH THE ONE I LOVE...

...WITH MY SPECIAL SOMEONE...

TRUP

TRUP

TRUP

TRUP

TRUP

NO MATTER WHICH SIDE OF YOU... IS OUT...

...TO ME YOU ARE ONE PERSON... AYA MIKAGE.

WHAT...

WAS HE FEELING THEN...?

TŌYA... HELD ME JUST LIKE THIS BEFORE...

YŪHI...

YŪHI, I AM **NOT** YOUR PERSONAL ENDTABLE! HOW AM I SUPPOSED TO WALK WITH THIS CUP ON MY HEAD?!

TŌYA!

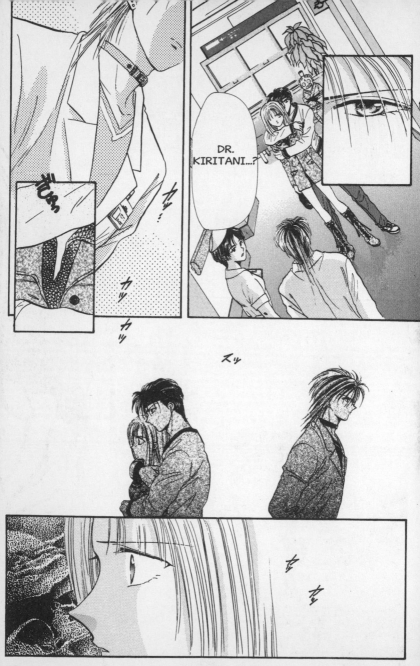

I JUST SEEM TO HAVE THE DEVIL'S OWN *LUCK!* AKI USED TO SAY DISASTERS WOULD RUN SCREAMING FROM ME!

PRETTY SNARKY, HUH?

OH, YOU BET! JUST SUPER DANDY, IN FACT! THANKS FOR ASKING!

BY THE WAY... I COULDN'T SAVE URAKAWA.

I SEE...

BUT THAT'S THE WAY IT'S GOTTA BE FROM NOW ON, I GUESS! IT'S CERTAINLY THE ONLY WAY I'LL BE ABLE TO STAND UP TO THE MIKAGES!

AND... SUZUMI WAS ATTACKED, SO I... LET *CERES* OUT! I PROBABLY... KILLED SOME PEOPLE.

IF YOU LOVE ME...

...HOLD ME IN YOUR ARMS, RIGHT NOW...!

PAGING DR. KIRITANI.

PLEASE REPORT TO INTERNAL MEDICINE, ROOM THREE.

...GO ON! I'M FINE.

YŪHI AND THE OTHERS ARE WAITING FOR ME ANYWAY.

JUST *GO!*

WHY... DID YOU COME TO TOCHIGI?

WHY DID *YOU*...?

OH!

C-GENOMES! IS *THAT* IT?! THE PEOPLE WHO WERE RECENTLY HOSPITALIZED... LIKE SHŌTA KURUMA...

THERE'S NO TELLING WHO WILL MANIFEST A FULL CELESTIAL ASPECT...

BUT MY ORDERS ARE TO BE READY TO CAPTURE ANYONE WHO DOES. THAT'S WHY I'M HERE.

DO *WHAT* PROPERLY?!

YOU NEED AT LEAST AN HOUR TO DO IT PROPERLY, START TO FINISH!

SHE'S TAKING HER *TIME!!*

CALM DOWN! IT'S ONLY BEEN 20 MINUTES!

NOTHING.

HMM...

WHAT'S SHE *SEE* IN THAT FREAK ANYWAY?!

I SHOULDN'T HAVE LET HER GO!

BASICALLY, AYA THINKS OF YOU AS JUST A FRIEND, WHILE YOU'RE COMPLETELY IN LOVE WITH HER!

WHAT DO YOU KNOW?!

HEY!

I KNEW IT!

SHOOMP

HUH?

I DIDN'T THINK OF GOING OUT TO LOOK FOR YOU UNTIL SHŌTA SAW THAT PICTURE A WEEK AGO. BUT I THINK YOU'RE REALLY *HOT*, YŪHI!

BUT THAT'S OKAY. ♥ *I'LL* BE YOUR GIRLFRIEND, NO PROBLEM!

GROAN

...By the way!
I've finally gotten hooked on Final Fantasy VII. ☺ When I was in bed with a cold and a high fever around New Year's, I got brainwashed (?) by all those commercials on TV, so I pre-ordered F.F. VII. I got it; but I hadn't touched it in six months... What? Why didn't I play it right away? I was busy with work, I moved, I just didn't have the time...and besides, I'd never played an RPG game before! Seriously! I owned F.F. III for the Super Nintendo, but back then, those games were so slow and boring, and I hated all the fighting and item management you had to do all the time. So even if though I gave it a try, I gave up on it right away. But this time, I was curious to see the graphics from the point of view of an artist—I thought I could learn something from it. I started playing F.F. VII and... "Hey, this is pretty cool. Ooh...This is interesting, what happens next? ...Geez, I'm totally hooked!"
It was all because I fell in love with Cloud. One of my friends also started playing, and we're both gaga over him. "Could you draw Cloud for me?" "Sure!" ...Do I really have the time for that?! Come to think of it, my editors (and my readers) think I'm a hard-core gamer because I've written about video games in my past columns. Sorry - I own very few games, and I don't play much. I have the SNES, PlayStation, and the Sega Saturn (my editor at the time got it for me for my birthday ♥). But I have fewer than 10 games in all. They were just collecting dust. There was a time when I was hooked on Street Fighter II(when it first came out), but I quickly lost interest. (I stopped playing fighting games because they hurt my drawing hand.) I play less than the average person. However, now I have awoken to their splendor! But I have so much work to do! Wh-what should I do...?
So now I just listen to the F.F. soundtrack...

YOU PEDOPHILE!

WHAT'S GOING ON HERE...?

SO LONG, SHŌTA! SEE YOU TOMORROW!

WE'LL BE IN TOWN FOR A WHILE, SO WE'LL DROP BY AGAIN, TOO. KEEP YOUR SPIRITS UP, OKAY?!

AYA! YOU'RE *BACK!*

A HOTEL? CAN WE GET ANYTHING WITHOUT A RESERVATION?

BUT HOW CAN I POSSIBLY *FULFILL* THEM?

OH BOY... LOOKS LIKE HE'S REALLY GOT HIS HOPES UP...

OKAY!

ALL WE HAVE TO DO IS FLASH THE AOGIRI BUSINESS CARD. THE NAME CARRIES A LOT OF WEIGHT!

◆ *Chidori* ◆

I ONLY GOT A LITTLE BANGED UP... THIS SCAR WAS...

...WHAT'S THE MATTER?

THEIR NECKS WERE BROKEN WHEN THEY TRIED TO *SHIELD* SHŌTA AND ME ...THEY DIED INSTANTLY! ...THAT'S HOW SHŌTA GOT HURT!

THEY WERE KILLED TWO YEARS AGO, WHEN A BUS WE WERE IN SKIDDED IN THE RAIN!

THAT'S MY MOM AND DAD!

OKAY, I'M OFF TO SNUGGLE UP WITH YŪHI. GOOD NIGHT!

GOOD NI--

I GUESS WE'VE BOTH SEEN SOME TOUGH TIMES...

HEH HEH...

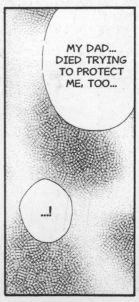

MY DAD... DIED TRYING TO PROTECT ME, TOO...

...!

C'MON, I WAS *KIDDING!!*

YANK

I HAD NO IDEA THESE KIDS HAD BEEN THROUGH SO MUCH TRAUMA.

I REALLY HOPE I CAN HELP SHŌTA...

...DR. KIRITANI.

DR. KIRITANI!

TRY NOT TO MAKE A HABIT OF SPACING OUT LIKE THAT. NOW, HERE ARE THE CHARTS FOR THE PATIENTS IN THE SPECIAL WING.

OH... RIGHT, I'M KIRITANI. SORRY.

EARTH TO DR. KIRITANI! COME IN, PLEASE!

BY THE WAY, YOUR BRONZE-COLORED HAIR IS A BIT GAUDY FOR THIS WORK ENVIRONMENT. *NO DOUBT IT'S ALL THE RAGE IN THE UNITED STATES, BUT...*

AND YOUR HAIR'S TOO LONG. YOU SHOULD CUT IT OR TIE IT BACK! AS FOR THOSE EARRINGS, OR WHATEVER THEY ARE...! *HEY, ARE YOU LISTENING?*

UH-HUH.

UH-HUH.

SHŌTA KURUMA

...

OH, DOCTOR... I'M OKAY... JUST A LITTLE ACHY.

IS THE SKY... INTEREST-ING?

I WAS IMAGINING... FAR OFF IN THE SKY SOMEWHERE... WHERE MY PARENTS ARE...

HI. I HEARD YOU'RE NOT FEELING WELL.

"OR ELSE... WELL, YOU KNOW!"

"I HAVE TO GO TO SCHOOL TODAY, SO VISIT SHŌTA WITHOUT ME!"

SHE'S SO... SO BRATTY... AND SHE'S THE LEAST OF MY PROBLEMS...

...SO YOU *STAY AWAY* FROM *THAT GUY!*

I'M TALKING ABOUT TŌYA!

OKAY.

AYA! MRS.Q AND I ARE GOING TO SEE WHAT WE CAN FIND OUT ABOUT THE PEOPLE WHO ARE HOSPITALIZED HERE...

MMBLE GRMBLE

COULD I GO THERE IF I COULD FLY? I MISS THEM...

I WANT TO SEE THEM AGAIN SO BAD...

HOW ABOUT YOUR PARENTS?

NEVER KNEW THEM...

YEAH, BUT... I STILL HAVE MY SISTER AND MY GRAND-PARENTS...

DON'T YOU... HAVE ANYBODY, DOCTOR?

I KNOW YOU'RE LONELY. WE ALL ARE, IN ONE WAY OR ANOTHER, FROM THE MOMENT WE'RE BORN TO THE DAY WE DIE.

SO I GUESS... IT WASN'T EASY GROWING UP?

NO, I DON'T.

I SUPPOSE IT WASN'T...

THEN... YOU'VE ALWAYS BEEN ALONE?

THAT MUST MAKE YOU SO SAD...

AND SCARED! I'D BE SCARED IF I WERE COMPLETELY ALONE!

UNTIL NOW... YOU SEE, I'VE FOUND SOMEONE.

YES, I'M SCARED... ALWAYS.

!

THAT'S GOOD! AND THAT MAKES YOU HAPPY?

BUT NOT SAD... BECAUSE YOU CAN'T MISS WHAT YOU'VE NEVER HAD. THERE'S NOTHING I MISS, NOTHING I'VE LOST, NOTHING I'VE EVER CARED ABOUT.

HEY, I KNOW! *I'LL* BE YOUR FRIEND! THEN YOU WON'T BE SO SAD...

DO YOU THINK... MAYBE *I'M* RUNNING AWAY...?

COULD I STOP AND FACE THINGS... LIKE YOU DO, DOCTOR?

REST NOW...

GET SOME SLEEP...

"THAT MUST MAKE YOU SO SAD..."

"...YOU'VE ALWAYS BEEN ALONE?"

MOMMY!

DADDY!

"I NEVER GET ANYTHING *DEFINITE* FROM YOU!"

"HOW CAN YOU LOOK AT ME LIKE YOU *DON'T CARE?!*"

BUT I WANT MORE AND MORE... I GET LONELY AND ANGRY FOR NO REASON...MY LONGING FOR HIM GROWS, AND DEEPENS.

I'D FLIRT WITH HIM LIKE A SILLY SCHOOLGIRL WITH A CRUSH, AND GET ALL GIDDY WHEN HE HUMORED ME A LITTLE.

I JUST WANTED A LITTLE EXCITEMENT AT FIRST.

...OR HOW HE HAS BEEN SUFFERING FOR MY SAKE.

THROUGH IT ALL, I'VE GIVEN NO THOUGHT TO *HIS* LONELINESS...

...AYA...

JUST LOOKING AT HIM, I'M OVERWHELMED BY HOW MUCH I LOVE HIM...
I UNDERSTAND NOW, TOYA...

YOU COULDN'T SAY
THE RIGHT WORDS
BECAUSE...

THEY DON'T EXIST.

YOU WON'T RUN, AND NEITHER WILL I.

EVERYONE SHOULD BE FATED TO KNOW A "BLISSFUL SUFFERING."

HOW WELL THAT DESCRIBES...
THE BITTERSWEET FEELING THAT COMES WHEN YOU LOVE SOMEONE...

...SO THESE ARE THE SEVEN PEOPLE HOSPITALIZED BECAUSE OF THE PATHOGEN?

THREE MEN AND FOUR WOMEN, INCLUDING SHŌTA. ALL DIFFERENT AGES... THE NUMBER OF CHILDREN THE TOCHIGI TENNYO HAD WAS ALSO...

...SEVEN...

96

NO MATTER WHAT I BECOME, MY FEELINGS WON'T CHANGE.

...I HAVE TO ACCEPT IT... NOT COWER AWAY FROM IT, NOT FIGHT AGAINST IT...

TO REJECT WHAT I AM... THAT WOULD JUST BE RUNNING AWAY.

THERE'S NOTHING TO BE AFRAID OF.

CERES IS PART OF ME, THAT'S HOW IT IS.

YOUR MISSION IS TO KILL ME, ISN'T IT? DIDN'T YOU SAY ANYONE WITH THE MIKAGES IS YOUR MORTAL ENEMY?

FWUMP

WHY AREN'T YOU TRYING TO CAPTURE ME? ISN'T THAT YOUR MISSION?

hm... I WAS THINKING OF AYA, AND HERE *YOU* ARE.

WHY DIDN'T YOU... TAKE AYA YESTERDAY?

ISN'T IT WHAT YOU MEN CONSIDER YOUR DUE, YOUR VERY *RIGHT?*

TO FIND OUT WHO, PERHAPS EVEN WHAT, YOU ARE...?

THAT WOULD BE... IRRESPON-SIBLE.

WHO... ARE YOU? I DON'T UNDERSTAND ANYTHING ABOUT YOU... YOU'RE A MYSTERY TO ME.

THAT MAKES TWO OF US. BEING ALONE IS SOMETHING I CAN LIVE WITH, BUT I WANT TO KNOW WHO I AM. I *NEED* TO KNOW.

THAT'S WHY I'M WITH THE MIKAGES.

DOCTOR, YOU'RE NEEDED *URGENTLY* IN THE ISOLATION WING! A PATIENT IS--!

beep

RRING

!

GRRRIP

YIKES!

KYŌKO... KYŌKO, HANG ON!

KYŌKO! CAREFUL THERE, THAT'S STARTING TO HURT!

NNGH!

YŪHI, WHAT *ARE* YOU BABBLING ABOUT?

OR MAYBE THERE'S SOME SIMPLE ROMANTIC TEEN COMEDY THAT NEEDS A LEAD...

I'M THROUGH!! A SMALL BIT ROLE, THAT'S ALL I NEED!!

WHAT DO YOU MEAN? YOU'RE ONE OF THE *MAIN CHARACTERS!*

THAT'S IT, I'M **DONE!** I'M JUST AN *EXTRA* IN THIS SHOW ANYWAY...

ACK!

IT... HURTS...

DR. KIRITANI!! THERE'S SOME KIND OF BARRIER, LIKE A WALL OF *ELECTRICITY*. WE CAN'T GET PAST IT...

YŪHI!!

STAND BACK. I'LL HANDLE IT.

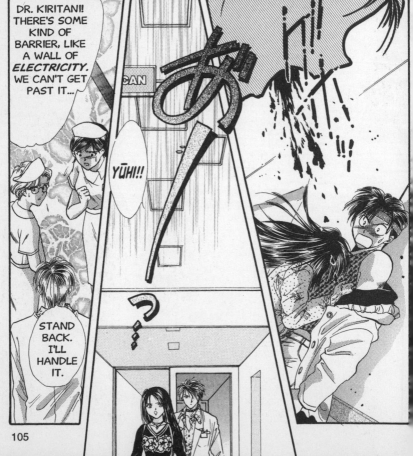

TOKYO...

YANK

!!

わあああ

KYOKO!

GO AHEAD... SAY WHATEVER YOU HAVE TO SAY. I'M JUST THE MIKAGES' LAPDOG, AFTER ALL.

UH... DOWN THE HALL, ON YOUR LEFT.

WHERE'S... THE BATHROOM?

HUF HUF

I FEEL JUST *HORRIBLE*, ALEC!

OKAY, AKI, NICELY DONE. HOW'RE YOU FEELING?

IT'S NOT LIKE *THAT* AT ALL! CERES IS THE MANIFESTATION OF A *CURSE* PUT ON THE MIKAGES, AND AYA'S JUST THE *VESSEL* FOR THAT CURSE!

BUT AYA NOT ONLY KNOWS ALL ABOUT HER PREVIOUS LIFE, SHE *TRANSFORMS* INTO IT!

YOU HAVE TO *REMIND* ME OF THAT?!

Oh yeah? BUT IT WAS YOU, IN YOUR PREVIOUS LIFE, WHO ANGERED CERES IN THE FIRST PLACE.

HOW IS ANYONE SUPPOSED TO KNOW WHAT THEY DID IN A PREVIOUS LIFE?!

AKI...

THAT'S WHY... I CAN'T SEE AYA ANYMORE...

I *HATE* THIS. PAST LIVES... REINCARNATION...

SIGH

I'M SORRY.

OH... IT'S NOT LIKE... I MEAN, I SHOULDN'T TAKE IT OUT ON *YOU*. THIS HASN'T BEEN A LOAD OF LAUGHS FOR YOU, EITHER...

HELLO?! YOU BEEN UNDER A *ROCK* THE PAST *COUPLE MONTHS?!*

IS SOMETHING BOTHERING YOU?

?

IT JUST SEEMS LIKE... WELL.... YOU SOUND LIKE A GUY WHO'S UPSET BECAUSE HE'S SEPARATED FROM HIS GIRLFRIEND.

ANYWAY, MY PROBLEMS ARE NOTHING COMPARED TO YOURS. YOUR WHOLE LIFE IS TURNING UPSIDE DOWN AND INSIDE OUT, WHILE I'M JUST... DOING MY JOB.

LEFT THEM ALL BEHIND. MY STUDIES AND MY RESEARCH ARE WHAT MY LIFE IS ABOUT. I DON'T NEED ANYTHING ELSE.

A QUEST THAT LED YOU TO *RELOCATE* TO JAPAN? WHAT ABOUT YOUR FAMILY, YOUR FRIENDS?

THERE ARE SIMILAR LEGENDS ALL OVER THE WORLD. I WAS DYING TO PROBE INTO THESE MYSTERIES, AND THE CHIEF SHARED MY PASSION. WE'VE BEEN ON A QUEST FOR ANSWERS EVER SINCE.

MAYBE YOU'RE RIGHT...

...

I'M SURE THEY CARE ABOUT YOU, AND DESERVE MORE ATTENTION FROM YOU THAN ANY ANCIENT MYSTERY.

CALL THEM. I BET THEY'RE WORRIED ABOUT YOU.

TECHNICAL JOURNALS AND MACHINES CAN'T LAUGH WITH YOU, WON'T CRY FOR YOU, AND WILL NEVER *LOVE* YOU.

I SHOULD TELL YOU... THE CHAIRMAN - YOUR GRANDFATHER - HAS BEEN IN POOR HEALTH LATELY.

WHAT?! WHY WASN'T I TOLD *SOONER?*

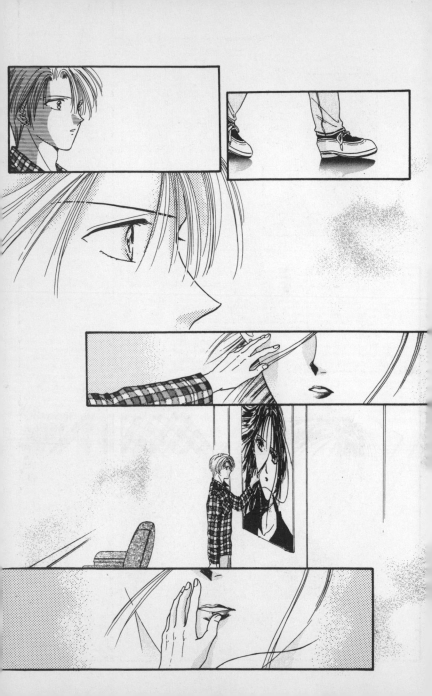

?!

GASP!

!!

MR. AKAGI HAS STOPPED BREATH-ING...

AND MR. SASAKI IS ALSO IN CRITICAL CONDITION...

THAT'S *FOUR*...

I'LL ENJOY WATCHING HOW THINGS DEVELOP BETWEEN YOU, YŪHI, AND AYA.

AND NOW, BACK TO YŪHI, THE THIRD PERSON IN THIS LOVE TRIANGLE...

ONLY THREE OF THEM ARE LEFT... KUMI AKIYAMA, HIROKAZU YOSHIZUKA...

...AND SHŌTA!

WELL, ALL THOSE "SPECIAL PATIENTS" *ARE* DROPPING LIKE FLIES...!

VICTIMS OF THOSE DAMN *MIKAGES!* THEY MUST BE HAVING NEGATIVE REACTIONS TO THE VECTOR MEDICATION!

KNOCK OFF THE NARRATION!

...WE FIND HIM INCAPACITATED. WOULDN'T IT BE OH-SO-PATHETIC, IF HE WERE TO MEET HIS END, CLUTCHING A BASIN FULL OF--

AND WHADDAYA MEAN "MEET HIS END?!"

CERES: 4

So I'm head over heels in love with Cloud. I seem to have a weakness for the strong silent type.

Sephiroth and Vincent too! Well, I've talked about how I love this character or that character before, but I don't want you to misunderstand. The way a creator "loves" a character and the way a reader "loves" a character are different. As their creator, my feelings include a bit of calculation - whether they are well developed, well drawn, or easy to draw. And I hope I wouldn't be so silly as to be infatuated with my own characters so much that I would lose sleep over them. If one of my characters were to come on to me, frankly, it would feel like incest and gross me out. ☺ I mean, they're like my children I gave **birth** to. That's why my "love" and a reader's "love" for my characters are totally different. Come to think of it, I once received a letter that told me I was "really fickle."

I chuckled to myself and thought, "It must be because I always have a different favorite character." Well, as I stated above, don't confuse it with **real** love. ☺ I'm actually very faithful. (Dare I say it myself?) Once I fall in love with someone, I cease to even think of other guys as "the opposite sex." ☺

For some reason, two of my editors once told me, "You seem like the devoted type," and I was freaked out. Um...why?! ☺

It's a little sickening to imagine myself that way, so at least I won't act that way in public. I tend to be tomboyish (I firmly believe I was a guy in my previous life.) so I don't understand girls sometimes. Maybe that's why my work is rather gender-neutral. At this rate, I wonder if I'll get more and more masculine... Don't worry! At least I haven't fallen in love with a woman yet! But I like to draw nude bodies...

Could it be...? hmm... Something left over from my previous life...???

But for now, I'll just settle for Cloud.

Cool men are the best!

HOW'S IT GOING, YŪHI?!

GUK?

I BROUGHT YOU A SNACK! IT'S A LOCAL SPECIALTY!

OKONO-MIYAKI*!!

CHIDORI! YOU JUST JUMPED RIGHT ONTO HIS QUEASY STOMACH. I THINK HE'S GOING TO--

TA DA

BY THE WAY, I JUST SAW AYA IN THE HALLWAY!

BWOOOR~

*CABBAGE PANCAKE TOPPED WITH MEAT, FISH FLAKES, SEAWEED, SPECIAL SAUCE, AND MAYONNAISE.

BUT I CAN SEE WHY. BEING UP HERE, LOOKING DOWN AT EVERYTHING AND EVERYBODY... IT MAKES ME WONDER WHY I'VE LET MYSELF BE SUCH A *WUSSY* ABOUT EVERYTHING!

SHE LEFT HER HUSBAND AND CHILDREN BEHIND. I GUESS HEAVEN MATTERED MORE THAN HER OWN FAMILY.

Um... THE STORY IS THAT SHE LOST HER HAGOROMO, BUT LATER FOUND IT AND RETURNED TO HEAVEN...

DADDY TOLD ME PEOPLE USED TO WORSHIP THE SKY BECAUSE IT'S SO BIG.

PEOPLE KNOW THEY MUST LIVE WITH THEIR FEET ON THE GROUND... SO THEY DESIRE WHAT THEY CANNOT REACH.

I WANT TO WALK...

...GROW UP STRONG... AND BECOME A *PILOT!*

BUT...

I STILL...

WANT TO FLY.

124

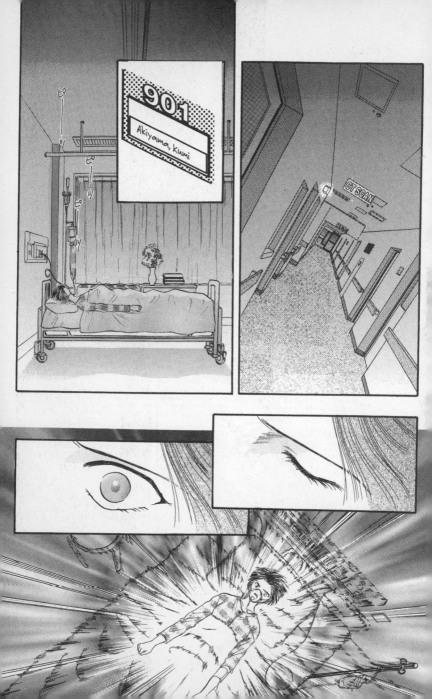

BIRTHDAY: September 5 (Virgo) Currently 25 years old

BLOOD TYPE: O

HEIGHT: 5'4" **BUST:** 34" **WAIST:** 24" **HIPS:** 34"

HOBBIES: Shopping, swimming

TALENT: Japanese traditional dance

SUZUMI AOGIRI

SHŌTA...!!

MOMMY...

SHŌTA!!

THIS *CAN'T* BE *HAPPENING!*

...

MOMMY...?

IT'S STRANGE, THOUGH... EVERYTHING AROUND ME... COLLAPSES.

HOW CAN I MAKE IT STOP...?

TP

TP

MISS AKIYAMA, YOU SHOULDN'T BE UP...

EVERY-ONE! GET *BACK,* NOW!!

I KNOW, BUT... I FEEL NEW *STRENGTH...* COURSING THROUGH MY BODY.

AYA! OH NO! ARE YOU--?

KUMI AKIYAMA'S CELESTIAL POWERS HAVE AWAKENED. THAT POWER CRUSHED...

NO, IT *IMPLODED* THEIR INTERNAL ORGANS. DOES THIS MEAN THE OTHER TWO, YOSHIZUKA AND SHŌTA, HAVE--?

DR. KIRITANI!!

OH MY!

WHAT HAPPENED HERE?!

MR. YOSHIZUKA'S GONE!

DAMMIT... WHAT'S GOING *ON* AROUND HERE...?

...MM...

AYA...!!

SHŌTA...

!

BUT IT WAS REALLY *MY* FAULT MORE THAN ANYONE'S...

HE'S CONVINCED IT WAS HIS FAULT OUR PARENTS DIED. HE THINKS...

BECAUSE THEY DIED TRYING TO PROTECT US...

WHAT?!

SHŌTA! WHERE'D HE GO?

DAD HAD A RARE DAY OFF... AND *I* WAS THE ONE WHO SUGGESTED WE GO TO A MOVIE!

I THREW A FIT LIKE SOME *SPOILED ROTTEN KID.* I SHOULD'VE LISTENED TO THEM...

MOM AND DAD DIDN'T THINK IT WAS A GOOD IDEA BECAUSE OF THE RAIN, BUT I INSISTED.

THAT'S WHY SHE'S SO OBSESSED WITH GETTING SHŌTA TO WALK AGAIN...

140

...NO NEED TO FEEL *EMBARRASSED* ABOUT THIS, AKI.

IT CAN'T BE... I DIDN'T EVEN REALIZE WHAT I WAS DOING.

THAT'S NOT WHAT I WAS--!

AND YOU CAN'T FACE BEING, SHALL WE SAY, *ROMANTICALLY* DRAWN TO YOUR LITTLE SISTER?

I DON'T THINK ANY LESS OF YOU.

IN FACT, I'M INTRIGUED. THE TWO OF YOU *WERE* A COUPLE IN YOUR PREVIOUS LIVES.

ON THE OTHER HAND, IN CERTAIN PARTS OF JAPAN THEY USED TO CALL MALE AND FEMALE TWINS "MARRIED CHILDREN" AND SHUNNED THEM BECAUSE IT WAS BELIEVED THEY WERE REINCARNATED LOVERS WHO COMMITTED LOVE SUICIDE IN THEIR PREVIOUS LIVES.

SOME CULTURES EVEN HAVE CREATION MYTHS...

IT'S NOTHING TO FRET ABOUT.

DID YOU KNOW THAT IN SOME COUNTRIES, TWINS ARE CONSIDERED TO BE A SPECIAL KIND OF LOVERS AND ARE CALLED "FIANCÉS"...?

IT BOILS DOWN TO THE FACT THAT, IN THIS WORLD, THERE ARE ONLY TWO TYPES OF LIVING BEINGS... MALE AND FEMALE.

...WHERE THE WORLD BEGINS WITH TWIN GODS, BROTHER AND SISTER. THEY HAVE CONJUGAL RELATIONS AND PRODUCE CHILDREN. HOW CAN WHAT YOU ARE FEELING BE CONSIDERED TABOO?

◆ Chidori ◆

So... This story arc is set in Tochigi, but Amago Village actually does exist. My editor videotaped footage there for me because I was too busy with work and couldn't go myself. (I cause him a lot of trouble ◯°)
There was an old lady there who claimed she was descended from a celestial maiden! My editor interviewed her, and she talked about Amago Village and how it may or may not have existed since the Jomon Period (approx. 13,000 - 300 B.C.). Wow, I guess tennyo really did exist. If we were to search all over Japan, I bet we'd find even more people of "celestial lineage." I mean, there's even a legend that Sugawara no Michizane (revered as the god of Academics) is descended from a tennyo. ...
W-Wait a minute...does this mean that little old lady is a C-Genome?! Actually, I heard a story about a guy (outside of Japan) whom DNA testing found to be a direct descendant of some stone age man—Cro-Magnon Man or something like that.
These days, you can find out just about anything from DNA. But get this, his wife commented, "Now I know why my husband likes his meat rare." What a sense of humor...
"HA HA HA"—Yes, that's how Americans really laugh! How can I say this? Because I just got back from vacation in Florida! It was actually supposed to be a trip to Arizona, but I thought, I might as well have some fun so I went to Disney World & Universal Studios! But the work just piled up while I was away! ☺ I'm tired, but I sure had a great time! There were rides that they don't have in Tokyo Disneyland, and they were so great! There's an alien ride called "EX" and it was so freaky! Things explode and water sprays on you, and you feel this warm breath on your neck... and then it's **right** behind you!! I was screaming my head off!

I wonder if it'll be coming to Japan anytime soon...

SHŌTA! DON'T **MOVE,** I'M COMING...

WAIT!

THE **SLIGHTEST JAR** COULD CAUSE THAT FLOOR TO COLLAPSE!

SHŌTA!

IF I WERE *CERES,* I COULD...

GOSH, WHAT A *LOUSY* TIME TO CHANGE INTO *ME!*

I'LL FIND A WAY TO GET TO HIM!

SHŌTA, LISTEN TO ME!

CRAWL OVER TO YOUR RIGHT! YOU SHOULD BE SAFE THERE, BUT BE *VERY* CAREFUL!

C'MON, SHŌTA, *MOVE...*

AND THAT'S HOW IT *SHOULD* BE!

I'M USELESS, AND NOW I'M GOING TO *DIE!*

NO! I *CAN'T* MOVE!

THINGS WOULD BE EASIER FOR YOU THEN, WOULDN'T THEY, CHIDORI?!

MOM AND DAD ARE DEAD, MY LEGS DON'T WORK, AND EVERYONE HAS TO LOOK AFTER ME! I *HATE* MY LIFE!

IF I DIE, I CAN FLY UP TO MOM AND DAD! THIS'LL ALL BE *OVER!*

HOW *OLD* DO YOU THINK YOU *ARE?!*

AYA!

YOU WHINING BABY!

148

◆ Chidori ◆

A-AND THE PEOPLE WHO LOVE YOU *WANT* TO HELP YOU...

AND THE NEXT TIME... *WE'LL* BE THERE TO HELP SOMEONE ELSE.

SOONER OR LATER, WE ALL NEED SOMEONE TO LEAN ON... SO WE ACCEPT THEIR HELP.

...LIKE CHIDORI... SHE BELIEVES IN YOU... SO *MUCH*...!

YŪHI!

HURRY... GET TO *SHŌTA* SOON!

149

THAT...

THAT WAS...

Chidori

In Disney World, I went to Magic Kingdom, MGM, and Epcot, and they were all great in different ways. But at Universal Studios, the big attraction was "Terminator 2 - 3D"!!!! ☺☺ It was incredible! We thought all the other rides were great, but they just paled in comparison. ☺

If you ever go, it's definitely a must-see!

You'll get goose bumps (I did!). When it was all over, everyone cheered and clapped! It was awesome. They built a Universal Studios in Osaka, and I wanted T2 to come to Japan, but the feature ride here is "Back to the Future"...

For certain reasons, I couldn't go on this ride, but my friend who **did** ride it said that after T2, it was "kinda lame." Well, I'll talk more about that next time...

Hmm, I talked about some serious stuff in the beginning of this volume, but it did relate to the manga. I had Chidori's character created even before serialization of **Ceres** started, and I have a lot of other characters lined up too.

I've visualized the story up to the end, but it continues to change a little bit all the time, so I don't really know what'll happen. And regarding Chidori, my assistant says Chidori is "yummy"...(?)

There are a lot of girl characters, unlike my previous title. But actually, the Mikages' side is mostly men. The structure of the story is men vs. women. There'll be a lot of significant developments in the next volume.

Maybe you'll even be shocked and surprised. (Although it's already been printed in serialized format.) We'll be getting into the crux of the story, so please don't miss it.

...But Tōya will still remain as mysterious as ever.

See you next time!

"Princess Mononoke" soundtrack playing in the background... 8/19/'97

UNH...!

DON'T MOVE!

SHŌTA!

159

160

?!

TŌYA?!

NO, I JUST KNOCKED HER OUT. I'M HERE TO CAPTURE, NOT KILL.

IS... IS SHE *DEAD?!*

THEN, SHE'S...

LOOKS LIKE THIS GIRL WON THE GAMBLE.

AFTER C-GENOMES ARE EXPOSED, IF THEIR BODIES ACCEPT THE VECTOR THEY AWAKEN TO THEIR CELESTIAL POWERS. IF THE VECTOR IS REJECTED, THEN THEY DIE.

A C-GENOME. THE MIKAGES CREATED A FALSE HEALTH EMERGENCY HERE, AND DISTRIBUTED THE VECTOR MEDICATION UNDER THE GUISE OF "TREATMENT."

!!

OOPS!

SHŌTA'S STILL IN *DANGER!*

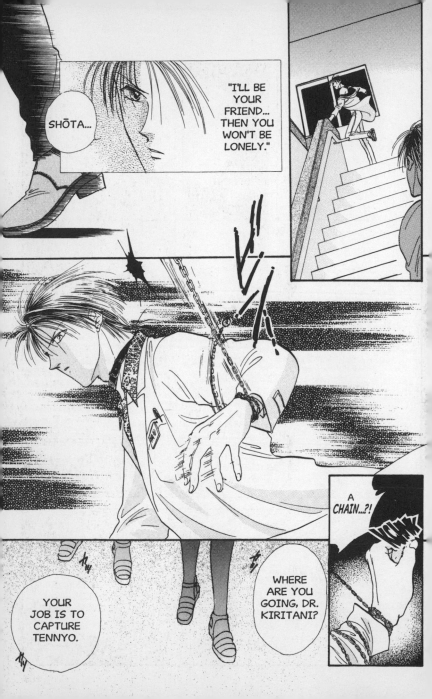

...OR YOU MAY BE SEEN AS A *TRAITOR*... TŌYA.

DON'T LET YOURSELF GET DISTRACTED FROM THAT...

SO *THAT'S* HOW IT IS.

I'M SURE YOU DON'T WANT *THAT*, RIGHT?

MIKAGE AGENTS SENT TO WATCH OTHER MIKAGE AGENTS...

BEEP

YAMAMINE HERE. SHŌTA KURUMA DIDN'T RESPOND TO THE VECTOR, BUT HIS *SISTER* DID! SHE'S ABOUT TO HAVE AN ENCOUNTER WITH C-GENOME YOSHIZUKA.

YES?

YŪHI!

UFF!

WHAT...

WHAT'S HAPPEN-ING TO ME...?

YOU *ASKED* FOR THIS!!

HUH?

HE NULLIFIED THE ATTACK...

TŌYA...

...HOW LONG WILL YOU GO ON DOING WHAT THE MIKAGES SAY, AND *HATING* YOURSELF FOR IT?

WHAT MEMORIES, WHAT *ANSWERS,* COULD POSSIBLY BE WORTH *THAT?*

MISS KUMI AKIYAMA.

...AKIYAMA...

HUH? WHERE... AM I? THIS ISN'T THE HOSPITAL...

THAT'S RIGHT, BUT DON'T BE AFRAID. THIS IS A PLACE FOR VERY SPECIAL PEOPLE LIKE YOU.

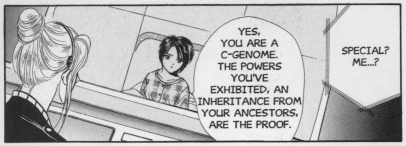

YES, YOU ARE A C-GENOME. THE POWERS YOU'VE EXHIBITED, AN INHERITANCE FROM YOUR ANCESTORS, ARE THE PROOF.

SPECIAL? ME...?

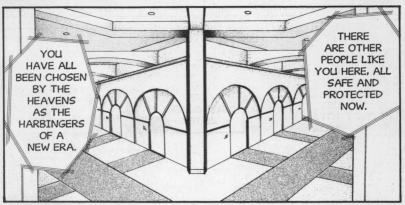

YOU HAVE ALL BEEN CHOSEN BY THE HEAVENS AS THE HARBINGERS OF A NEW ERA.

THERE ARE OTHER PEOPLE LIKE YOU HERE, ALL SAFE AND PROTECTED NOW.

THIS MAKES SIX TENNYO THAT HAVE COME TOGETHER.

HAVING AWAKENED TO YOUR TRUE SELVES, YOUR SUFFERINGS ARE FINALLY OVER.

FOR NOW, REST, AND REGAIN YOUR STRENGTH.

...

BUT NO ONE LIKE AYA OR CHIDORI KURUMA.

NONE OF THE OTHER C-GENOMES HAVE UNDERGONE *COMPLETE* CELLULAR TRANS-FORMATION.

PERHAPS. BUT WE *WILL* ACQUIRE CHIDORI KURUMA AND CERES SOONER OR LATER.

OUR SIX MIGHT DEVELOP SIMILAR RESPONSES, GIVEN TIME...

IN THE MEANTIME... WE MUST SHOW TŌYA THE *ERROR* OF HIS WAYS...

TO BE CONTINUED...

The Ceres Guide to Sound Effects

We've left most of the sound effects in CERES as Yuu Watase originally created them – in Japanese.

VIZ has created this glossary to help you decipher, page-by-page and panel-by-panel, what all those foreign words and background noises mean. Use this guide to impress your friends with your new Japanese vocabulary.

The glossary lists the page number then panel. For example, 3.1 is page 3, panel 1.

23.3 FX: Biku (flinch)	5.3 FX: Doki… (ba-bump)
24.5 FX: Doki (ba-bump)	6.6 FX: Furu furu (tremble)
25.3 FX: Dokun dokun (ba-bump ba-bump)	9.3 FX: Gyu… (squeeze)
27.5 FX: Kacha (kachook)	10.1 FX: Ga (grip)
	10.2 FX: Bikun (shudder)
29.3 FX: Gaa (automatic door)	10.6 FX: Gyu… (clench)
29.4 FX: Katsu (tump)	
	12.4 FX: Za (slash)
30.4 FX: Kashan (clack)	
	13.5 FX: Poto… (plop)
31.2 FX: Ga (stab)	
31.5 FX: Kiri (cutting)	14.5 FX: Niko… (smile)
	15.1 FX: Ka ka ka (tup tup tup)
	15.2 FX: Ka ka ka (tup tup tup)
	16.1 FX: Gako (shup)
	17.6 FX: Ni (smirk)
	18.1 FX: Fan fan (weeoo weeoo)
	20.1 FX: Paa (fwish)
	20.4 FX: Gyu (clench)

104.1 FX: Piku (twitch)
104.5 FX: Suu (slide)

105.1 FX: Fura (stagger)
105.2 FX: Gu (urp)
105.3 FX: Geho (cough)
105.4 FX: A—!! (augh)

106.1 FX: Su (passing through)
106.3 FX: Zuru (slip)
106.4 FX: Tata (tup)

107.1 FX: Waaah (sob)

108.4 FX: Beki (smash)

112.4 FX: Kyu… (squeak)

116.6 FX: Katsu… (tump)

119.3 FX: Kasha (click)

120.1 FX: Piku (flinch)

121.1 FX: Doki doki (ba-bump ba-bump)

125.3 FX: Pi— pi— pi— (beep beep)

126.2 FX: Guwa (crash)

130.5 FX: Ga (slam)

131.4 FX: Bata bata (running)

132.1 FX: Zawa zawa (murmur murmur)

134.2 FX: Gachi (clench)

75.5 FX: Ira ira (pacing)

76.1 FX: Kasha (click)

78.4 FX: Niko (smile)

79.2 FX: Doh (donk)

81.1 FX: Gashi (hug)
81.1 FX: Ton ton (chop chop)
81.2 FX: Zakkuri (slice)
81.3 FX: Pasha (click)

83.6 FX: Niko (smile)

85.3 FX: Kotsu… (step)

86.4 FX: Takumo— (sheesh)

90.5 FX: Su (reaching hand)
90.6 FX: Chichichi (chirp chirp)

91.1 FX: Suu (drawing hand away)

96.3 FX: Don (slam)
96.4 FX: Buru buru (shudder shudder)
96.5 FX: Bibi (bzzt)

97.1 FX: Bachi bachi (zap crackle)

99.4 FX: Zaku zaku (hair flowing)
99.5 FX: Ga (grab)

100.1 FX: Za (fwoosh)

103.5 FX: Ban (smash)
103.5 FX: Pari—n (clink)

Yuu Watase was born on March 5 in a town near Osaka, Japan, and she was raised there before moving to Tokyo to follow her dream of creating manga. In the decade since her debut short story, "Pajama De Ojama" (An Intrusion in Pajamas), she has produced more than 50 compiled volumes of short stories and continuing series. Watase's beloved works *CERES: CELESTIAL LEGEND*, *IMADOKI!* (*Nowadays*), *ALICE 19TH*, *ABSOLUTE BOYFRIEND*, and *FUSHIGI YŪGI: GENBU KAIDEN* are now available in North America in English editions published by VIZ Media.

If you like
CERES: CELESTIAL LEGEND,
here are some other manga
VIZ recommends you read:

© 2001 Yuu Watase/Shogakukan, Inc.

ALICE 19TH is the latest North American release from Yû Watase. Alice Seno is an ordinary high school girl living in the shadow of her older sister, Mayura. When a magical rabbit literally jumps into Alice's life, she quickly learns about the power of words. When Mayura is accidentally cast into a world of darkness, Alice must become a Lotis Words master in order to save her sister.

© 1992 Yuu Watase/Shogakukan, Inc.

FUSHIGI YÛGI is Yû Watase's popular fantasy shôjo series about a junior high school girl who suddenly travels to a fictional version of ancient China, where she finds love, betrayal and adventure.

VIDEO GIRL AI © 1989 by MASAKAZU KATSURA/SHUEISHA Inc.

VIDEO GIRL AI is a twist on the traditional love triangle. Yota Moteuchi's heart is broken when he finds out the girl he's in love with is in love with his friend. He wanders into a mysterious video store and picks up a rental starring cute, young Ai Amano. When he pops the tape into his broken VCR, Ai jumps from the screen into Yota's arms.

GET THE COMPLETE
FUSHIGI YÛGI COLLECTION

Hot Gimmick™

Will our hapless heroine ever figure out the game of love? Find out in *Hot Gimmick*— get the complete collection today!

Read the original manga—all 12 volumes available now

A novelization of the popular manga, with alternate ending and a bonus manga episode!

From the creator of *Tokyo Boys & Girls*— available from our Shojo Beat Manga line

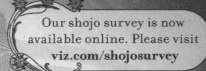